THE AUT]

Brian Sm

GW00384063

Holds the record for the fas
ings of the Lyke Wake Walk over the North York ...
pleted the 210miles over rough terrain on 5 crossings in June 1995
taking 85hours and 50minutes.

Brian lectures on outdoor pursuit courses and between
these travels extensively on walking expeditions and projects
around Great Britain.

Long distance running and canoeing are other sports he
enjoys, completing 25 marathons and canoeing the Caledonian
Canal 3 times.

His most recent venture involved cycling from Lands End
to John O`Groats in August 2001, a journey of over 900miles in
6days 13hours 18minutes. This involved carrying food, clothing
and tent, and was completed without any support between both
ends.

First Published 2002
ISBN 1-903568-07-2

Published by Challenge Publications,
7 Earlsmere Drive, Barnsley S71 5HH

CONTENTS   Page

THE ISLE OF WIGHT
NORTH TO SOUTH - EAST TO WEST

2 WALKS of
18 & 28 Miles
Across the Isle of Wight

An Essential guide to
help you complete
these Isle of Wight walks

Brian Smailes

You will never walk alone with these books published by
Challenge Publications

Top Ten Series

THE YORKSHIRE DALES TOP TEN
ISBN 0-9526900-5-5

THE LAKELAND TOP TEN
ISBN 0-9526900-3-9

THE DERBYSHIRE TOP TEN
ISBN 1-903568-03-X

Other books by the same author

THE SCOTTISH COAST TO COAST WALK
ISBN 0-9526900-8-X

17 WALKS IN GLEN NEVIS
ISBN 1-903568-05-6

THE COMPLETE ISLE OF WIGHT COASTAL FOOTPATH
ISBN 1-903568-08-0

JOHN O'GROATS TO LANDS END
ISBN 0-9526900-4-7

THE NATIONAL 3 PEAKS WALK
ISBN 0-9526900-7-1
Also on CD

THE NOVICES GUIDE TO THE LYKE WAKE WALK
ISBN 0-9526900-1-2

THE YORKSHIRE 3 PEAKS WALK
ISBN 1-903568-01-3

THE 1066 COUNTRY WALK
ISBN 1-903568-00-5

MILLENNIUM CYCLE RIDES IN 1066 COUNTRY (EAST SUSSEX)
ISBN 1-903568-04-8

ISBN1-903568-07-2
FIRST PUBLISHED 2002
CHALLENGE PUBLICATIONS
7, EARLSMERE DRIVE, BARNSLEY. S71 5HH
www.chall-pub.fsnet.co.uk
E mail challengepublications@yahoo.co.uk

INTRODUCTION

This book covers two main routes crossing the centre of the island, north to south and east to west and consists of 18miles and 28miles of very scenic countryside.

Should you have perhaps walked the coastal footpath of the Isle of Wight then these walks across the centre of the island are a must if you want to complete your tour of this island.

The East to West route, from Bembridge to the Needles, is very impressive and will provide lasting memories of your visit to the Isle of Wight. The final section to the Needles will give you an exciting climax to your walk across the island.

Each route is divided into two sections to enable you to walk at a leisurely pace and have time to stop and visit the attractions on route. Overall both routes should take four days, walking at a steady pace but can be completed in two days by making an early start and a late finish.

Throughout both routes you will pass numerous cafes, public houses and shops where refreshments can be purchased. The main towns and villages as you would expect have numerous public houses but I have not mentioned them individually. Where you pass others on route, these are shown in the useful information section.

Wherever you are on these walks you will not be far away from a house, farm or village in an emergency. Compass bearings generally are not necessary as there are many public footpath signs throughout both routes. Where bearings are helpful then these are shown. Grid references are given at various points in the route descriptions to enable you to pinpoint the exact route and to help find more difficult areas or places on the map.

All public footpath signs herein are referred to as P.F. often followed by a number. Enjoy this walk as I did and go on to complete the coastal footpath if you have not already done so.

Public transport is generally available to take you back to your base each day. Most buses travel to Newport and there are connections from the bus station there to all parts of the island. It is advisable to check bus times before you leave each day and plan your day accordingly.

THE ISLE OF WIGHT

This island may be relatively small, measuring approximately 23miles by 13miles, at the widest points but it holds a wealth of treasures. There are Castles, Stately Homes, Manor Houses, Abbeys and Churches as well as excellent scenery throughout, especially over Tennyson Down, St. Catherine's Point and Bembridge Down, to name but a few. Over 600miles of footpaths and bridleways cover the island, enabling walkers to experience the delights of the varied landscape.

The island was once part of the mainland, about 6000B.C. but the sea gradually encroached on the area as the ice sheets melted, producing the island we see today. Stone Age man were inhabitants here, also Bronze Age man with their barrows and ditches, and more recent visitors, the Romans who left villas in Newport and Morton.

Christianity came to the island in the 7th century, and a few hundred years later the influence of William the Conqueror brought about the building of Carisbrooke Castle. The crown has owned the island since 1293. Queen Victoria built Osborne House here in 1845 as her holiday retreat.

Alfred, Lord Tennyson had a home here and a cross is erected on Tennyson Down near the Needles to mark his life and achievement as the Poet Laureate.

Newport is the principal and most central town on the island. There are also a number of resorts and villages situated around the coastline. Inland there are a number of small villages and a network of roads giving access to all parts.

Being an island many of the population have boats and enjoy work and leisure pursuits connected with the sea. Yarmouth harbour is a fine example of sea faring tradition and a busy harbour for pleasure boats throughout the summer months.

There are many attractions here for visitors and those you pass on these routes are mentioned in this book, should you wish to visit them. You will undoubtedly find the local people are friendly, helpful and welcoming to everyone.

ACCESS TO THE ISLAND

Portsmouth to Ryde
Wightlink: Fast Cat/Ferry	0870 5827744
Hovercraft	01983 811000
High Speed Catamaran	0870 5827744

Portsmouth to Fishbourne
Wightlink Ferry	0870 5827744

Southampton to Cowes
Red Funnel Ferry	023 80334010

Lymington to Yarmouth
Wightlink Ferry	0870 5827744

EQUIPMENT

To enable you to enjoy this walk, I recommend the following clothing/equipment items. Depending on whether you are attempting separate day walks or the full route, you may need to add or delete some items on this checklist: -

1. Waterproof/Windproof Jacket
2. Small Tent/Sleeping Bag
3. Cooking Stove/Fuel/Matches
4. Pans/Cutlery/Plate/Cup/Food/Water Bottle
5. Sunscreen/Insect Repellent
6. Boots and Trainers/spare socks
7. Rucksack/Day Sack
8. Gloves/Hat
9. Suitable Trousers (not jeans)
10. First Aid Kit/Whistle/Survival Bag
11. Torch/Spare Bulb/Batteries
12. Map/Compass/pencil/notepad
13. Spare Clothing
14. Toiletries

Most importantly do not walk in high heels and/or jeans and T-shirt because you will quickly get aching or blistered feet and no doubt feel cold. Jeans can chafe the skin and take a long time to dry if wet as well as drawing the body heat.

Select your equipment carefully and you will feel the benefit when walking or camping.

A large percentage of the North to South route is on metalled track/path so you may find it easier on the feet to walk in trainers, changing into boots for the fields and off road sections.

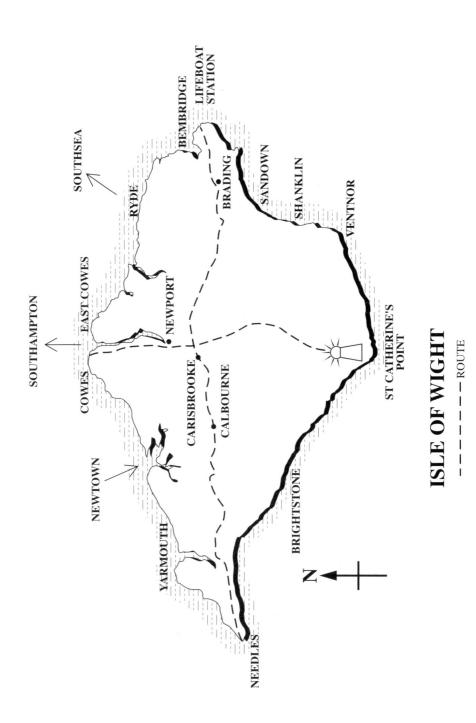

ISLE OF WIGHT

– – – ROUTE

N

THE ROUTES

North to South - Cowes to St Catherine's Lighthouse
Time to Allow 9.5hrs
Total Distance 17.7miles (28.6 km)
Start G.R. 494966

Leaving from the Royal Yacht Squadron at the entrance to the River Medina in Cowes, (Plate 1) walk along Bath Road towards the centre of the town, onto Shooters Hill then Birmingham Road. At the end of Birmingham Road, cross to a pub called The Duke of York then walk along York Street which is at the right side of the pub.

At the far end of York Street, cross onto Pelham Road and near the end turn right into South Road then left onto Arctic Road. You come to a mini roundabout near a gravel works. Look for a cycling and P.F. sign pointing to Newport 3½miles. Cross onto the long straight path, which runs parallel with the River Medina to Newport.

You eventually come to a roundabout on the industrial estate where a sign points to Newport town centre. Continue through the industrial estate then walk under the bridge carrying the main dual carriageway above. At the mini roundabout on the far side, turn right onto Hunnycross Way.

Pass Sainsburys fuel station on your right walking to a set of traffic lights. Turn left towards the statue in the town centre with the lion figures around it. Continue straight across on St. Johns Place G.R. 498892, passing shops then Node Hill middle school on your left, now at the far side of the town centre. Keep in the same direction along St. Johns Road.

5   At the mini roundabout ahead a sign states 'Shide Road' to your left. Descend the hill 500m to The Barley Mow pub in Shide. Do not take the first P.F. sign off to the right, but just past the pub, a P.F./cycle sign points to Blackwater 1mile. This track runs parallel with a stream on your left and the road nearby.

6   Just before Blackwater cross a narrow wooden bridge to emerge on a lane. Turn left, walking for 100m to a main road. Turn right, walk round a left-hand bend G.R. 506862, then take the 2nd P.F. on your left at the end of the houses 350m further on which is the Stenbury Trail.

7   Just after passing 'Little Birchmore' G.R. 516853, the metalled track becomes a small stone track. Follow this farm track to a crossing between the fields. A public bridleway sign points in the same direction towards Pagham.

8   You come to some farm buildings at Pagham, bear left in front of the houses then right on a track at the side, bearing 241°M, which winds round to the left to a main road near some houses 700m away. Now follow a P.F. sign to Kennerley Heath, walking to the right of the houses opposite on a short concrete track then through an opening into a field.

*A bus stop is situated outside the houses at G.R. 515837. Here you can divide your walk into two days and use a bus to get back to Newport (bus station).

9   Cross this field looking for the slightly worn path. Ahead you should see a tower in the distance. This is Hoy's Monument on St. Catherine's Hill (Plate 2) and you pass by it just before Niton. If in doubt then keep in the general direction of this tower.

Descend a short steep hill crossing two stiles, following the small direction arrows over the next two fields and passing a farm. Bear right after the next field, which is on the lower ground, then ascend to Elliot's Hill and the main road at G.R. 510834.

Walk with care along the road towards Chequers Inn. A further 320m is a sign for East Appleford Farm. Turn onto a P.F. GL9 signed 'The Wilderness and Cridmore'. Go through a small metal gate then turn left (do not carry on towards the wood). You should be heading towards the monument on the hill in the distance, (Plate 2) bearing 174°M from the gate.

Walk alongside the hedge on your left on a part sand path then onto a stony farm track. The hill is directly in front now. On reaching a main road, turn right walking for 750m. Turn left off the main road towards Upper Appleford Farm. Follow the lane round to two metal gates, which are opposite each other. Do not go through but continue on the lane walking clockwise passing Upper Appleford Farm G.R. 495801.

Ascend the brow of a short hill then just over the brow take the first turning left, along a narrow tree lined path towards the monument. Go through a wooden gate with a sign stating 'Please Shut Gate', onto a path alongside a field as you start to ascend the side of the hill, in an area known as 'The Rew'.

You come to a place with two metal gates enclosed in a square pen. Turn left and ascend through the wood. Go through a small metal gate, still ascending, on to a narrow path for 600m to the base of St. Catherine's Hill (Plate 2). Walk through another metal gate and bear right towards Hoy's Monument. The path divides, take the higher one.

15 Walk along the top of the hill, G.R. 495786, which has commanding views in all directions, towards a radio/T.V. mast at the far end. Cross a stile before reaching the mast then bear left on a track to Niton, bearing 128°M from the gate there.

16 Take the 2nd P.F. leading off to the right G.R. 500775, to descend the hill (Bury Path). Eventually you descend Pan Lane to come to the church of St. John in Niton. Turn right, walking in front of the church, for 400m to the far end of the houses on the left where a P.F. sign NT33 states 'Boxers Lane and Coastal Path'.

17 Walk along the narrow grass path into a field, going across it, to a stile into another field. There are good views in all directions here. Continue along by the wire fence, go over another stile, and then turn left descending to the main road.

18 Turn right, on a slight descent, towards St. Catherine's Point, walking on a lane passing between 'No Entry' signs. You pass some houses on your left while descending the hill. A P.F. sign is on your left, follow this to Sandrock Road emerging at Buddle Inn.

19 Turn right by the front of the inn then left on a P.F. descending some steps towards St. Catherine's Lighthouse. At the bottom of the steps, turn right on to a stone path. This path winds round in front of a café and some caravans then onto a section of National Trust land marked Knowles Farm.

20 You emerge on the cliff-top with St. Catherine's Lighthouse ahead. Continue on the cliff path to the wall around the lighthouse.

You have completed the North to South crossing of the island. Congratulations!

East to West - Bembridge to The Needles
Time to Allow 12hrs
Total Distance 27.7miles (44.5 km)
Start G.R. 656881

Your East to West route starts beside the lifeboat station in Bembridge (Plate 3). Walk along the main street leading away from the lifeboat station, for 900m to the junction. You see a sign 'Steyne Road', bear left along this road. At the next junction, known as Steyne Cross, turn right at the mini roundabout following the signs to Bembridge windmill.

On a slight left hand bend you see Bembridge windmill behind some trees. On the next right hand bend, turn left following the sign to the windmill, 120m further. Just as you approach, bear right walking behind the windmill (Plate 4). Cross a stile where a P.F. sign BB21 points to Brading. You should see it in the distance, 3km ahead.

Enjoying the good views over the surrounding area and walking on the Bembridge Trail, go over another four stiles descending towards the corner of an airfield you should see ahead. A sign states 'Beware of low flying aircraft'. Cross the airfield on an obvious path leading to a stile between the hedges.

Walk across a field to another stile on an obvious path towards Brading, which you should soon see again. The path twists around a field before passing through a narrow archway of bushes and a small wood. Keep on the main path following signs to Brading. If you do stray off the path in this area look ahead for Brading and re-orientate yourself back to the path.

11

The path twists to the right of Brading, passing the church, which you may see, in the distance. You come to a small wooden bridge over a stream but keep to the right hand path and walk towards the white painted house at G.R.613873 going through a kissing gate. Walk along Wall Lane to the junction beside the church.

Turn left on the busy road then cross, turning right along a narrow street called Cross Street between two 'No Entry' signs. Turn right at the top of the lane, walking along a narrow footpath for 320m to a main road where another P.F. sign B27, points left to Brading Down.

Ascend the right side of a field to a wood. Turn right on a good path along the lower right side of the wood. Go through a metal gate then ascend bearing left over the hillside on The Nunwell Trail. There are good views in all directions here.

Pass through a five bar gate before coming to a busy road. Turn right here walking on the road, with care, over the brow of the hill then descend until you see the 2nd P.F. sign just past a short left-hand bend. A white monument (sea mark) is on a hill ahead.

The P.F. sign points to Alverstone B33. Descend to a farm, passing through a five bar gate. Bear right at the far side of the farm on a short stretch of metalled road. On your left is a P.F. sign to Niton. Turn left here descending a winding path through a metal gate.

Walk by the side of a field and a quarry on the main path, which skirts the quarry. On meeting a wide track, go across on the winding path to arrive at the entrance to Lower Niton Farm 650m further on then bear right on the metalled road. Continue to a T-junction, go straight across to the far side of two houses then turn left on the Bembridge Trail again.

Plate 1
The start of the North to South Route
at the Royal Yacht Squadron in Cowes

Plate 2
View looking towards Hoy's Monument
and St. Catherine's Hill near to the end of the
North to South Route

Plate 3
The start of the East to West Route
at Bembridge Lifeboat Station

Plate 4
Bembridge Windmill on the
East to West Route

Plate 5
Passing Carisbrooke Castle
on the East to West Route

Plate 6
Passing Nodes Point Beacon
near the Needles on the
East to West Route

A P.F. sign NC7 points to Mersley Down & Arreton. Walk on this good grass path, which is on the left side of a field. Cross a stile and another field before going alongside a fir tree plantation. The path then winds round to your left where you should see a house. Walk towards the house and the minor road just beyond it.

Walk in front of the house for 50m, turning right on a track (no signpost) which has a gentle descent. Keep on this obvious track of sand and gravel in a westerly direction walking towards the T.V. mast, which you should see ahead at the top of a hill.

You approach a place called Craft Village, which you now see ahead of you. A track known as Shepherds Lane crosses your path. You turn right here then left following the public bridleway sign pointing to Arreton A9. Walk on this farm track, to the main A3056 road passing St George's Nursery.

Turn right at the busy main road, taking extreme care. Walk on the footpath where possible passing The White Lion pub. At a sharp bend in the road (Arreton Cross), a sign points to East Cowes and Ryde. Turn right here then immediately left following a P.F. sign St George's Down and Newport.

You are now walking along a dusty track where you come to four P.F. signs but continue in the same direction signed Newport. You come to a wide gravel path as you approach a gravel works. You soon pass a golf course on your right and gravel pits on the left. Cross the entrance to the quarry and golf club. There are a number of quarries along this lane. A steep descent on St George's Lane is ahead as you enter Shide and emerge at the busy A3020 main road.

Cross with care, walking past the Barley Mow pub on your right side. Continue in a straight line ascending the lane (B3401) to cross a mini roundabout. Pass houses on both sides, still on a slight ascent. At the brow of the hill you see a P.F. sign N24 bearing left to Carisbrooke Castle.

Turn here, between the houses, then follow a P.F. sign bearing right to ascend between the small trees on each side. You emerge on a path between some fields; there are excellent views to your right of Newport and the surrounding area and the River Medina. You are now on a good grass path as you pass a 'trig' point in a field to your left (marking the highest ground) known as Mount Joy.

A cemetery is on your right as you descend a flight of steps to a road. Turn left then immediately right following the P.F. sign for Carisbrooke Castle. Now you are walking around the outside of the castle walls (Plate 5) in a clockwise direction to the car park at the far side.

*On reaching the car park entrance, this point is a convenient place to end this day's walk, where public transport is available to Newport (bus station) then on to your base on the island.

Continuing to The Needles from here, look for the P.F. sign N88 at the car park entrance pointing to Millers Lane. Descend then bear right on to Clatterford Shute (lane). After passing 'Badmington' house, turn left onto P.F. N104 to Bowcombe. Cross a stile and footbridge, walking for 1.6km following a narrow worn path through the fields, generally keeping parallel with Luckley Brook

Cross several stiles keeping by the hedge then you emerge onto a track near Bowcombe Farm. Turn left on the lane then right soon after to a small wood called Frogland Copse. Keep to the right of the wood descending to the B3323 road. Cross this busy road with care. A public bridleway is opposite, which ascends steeply on a chalk path to the top of the hill. At a crossroads in the track bear left, G.R. 461859, on a gradual ascent.

Walk through the five bar gate still ascending over the brow of the hill. You should see a T.V. mast ahead as you come to another crossroad at G.R. 457858. Continue along the path, which gradually bears right towards the mast. On reaching another cross-roads with five signposts, take the left path marked Brightstone Forest.

Continue for 900m to the corner of Brightstone Forest where you can clearly see the T.V. mast to your right. At the corner of the forest go through a small metal gate beside a five bar gate then bear right on a track leading to Calbourne, bearing 318°M from the gate, (do not go along by the forest).

You should be walking alongside a field with a fence and hedge to your right. There are good views of the sea ahead and to your right. You come to three signposts together at Swainstondown Gate and to the left of them is a small gate, which you go through. Now you descend a hill on a track, passing sheep enclosures on your left near the bottom. Keep to the path.

There is a wood at the bottom of the hill, walk to the right of it on a good grass field then track. Pass over two cattle grids on your way to New Barn Farm buildings then onto the main road. Turn left walking for 650m to the crossroads in Calbourne. Pass the Sun Inn on your right at the crossroads.

Continue straight on, walking round a left-hand bend on the B3401 to descend to Calbourne Water Mill on your right. Look for a P.F. CB11B to Newbridge, which takes you through the car park at Calbourne Mill. Cross a stile at the far end of the car park and keep right, walking on a narrow path at the side of the fence into another field.

Cross a stile on your right then follow a winding path through a wood. At a fork in the path, take the left one with a yellow arrow and HT written on a small sign. Go over a small wooden bridge where your path winds through and out of the wood on the other side.

Cross a field, on a worn path, to emerge at a junction of three P.F. A sign points to Eades Farm, which you can see ahead. Take P.F. S23 signed Dodpits Lane ¾ mile. Go over a stile next to the sign for Eades Farm, walking alongside the field keeping the trees to your right, G.R. 407870.

You can see the farmhouses ahead as you cross two stiles, staying by the side of the field. Before you climb to the brow of the small hill, cross a stile to your left. This takes you through a short section of wood then into a large field. Keep left by the wood for 100m then bear right across the field and onto Dodpits Lane then turn left.

A P.F. sign S34 is on the right, follow this to Churchills Farm and Broad Lane, for 2.2km. You are now walking on a narrow concrete road to the farm. Continue in this same direction now crossing large fields in a straight line. You should see a radio mast ahead, follow the path, which eventually takes you close by the mast on the left side.

You see two signposts but continue straight ahead in the direction of a large farm building. A sign states Broad Lane but continue to the farm building. Cross two stiles near the farm to walk between the farm buildings on a concrete road. Pass several houses, to descend to the road at Tapnell Cottages.

Turn right on the two way metalled road for 650m where a P.F. sign on your right points across a field to a small wood. Go into the field walking to the far corner of the wood 400m further. Walk around the wood to the far corner then diagonally across the field bearing 306°M from the corner of the wood to join another P.F. Bear 256°M across the field to a small opening in the hedge.

Go through and you should see the greenhouses of a fruit farm on your right as you walk past a row of trees to emerge on Wilmingham Road. A public bridleway sign F25 points to The Causeway ½mile. Take this narrow path, which goes between a hedge and a fence.

There are some houses ahead as you approach a minor road. Turn left on the metalled road, walking to the converted barns, to join the main Newport road at the junction. Turn right on the B3399 towards Freshwater Bay walking for 360m to Afton Road.

Follow a sign 'Freshwater', going straight across onto Blackbridge Road and passing Afton Marsh Nature Reserve. Stay on the winding lane to emerge beside St Agnes' church. Turn left to P.F. F46 Tennyson Down & Needles, just past the bus shelter.

Walk through a kissing gate, on a gradual ascent on an obvious path between two hedges. Ascend alongside a small field to go through a five bar gate. You are now on a gradual ascent by the side of woodland for 2.2m going towards The Needles in a westerly direction.

You come to the remains of a quarry, continue slowly upwards to Nodes Point Beacon, (Plate 6) where a sign points in the same direction to The Needles. This is the final section of your walk, on a chalk path over the down.

There are excellent views in all directions from here. Leave the coastguard cottages to your left as you cross the stile onto the road, walking to the viewpoint a short distance away which is the end of your journey.

Congratulations, you have walked East to West across the Isle of Wight!

USEFUL INFORMATION

Attractions

East to West
1   Bembridge Lifeboat Station
2   Bembridge Shipwreck & Maritime Museum
3   Bembridge Windmill
4   Isle of Wight Waxworks
5   Lilliput Museum of Antique Dolls & Toys
6   Robin Hill Country Park
7   Guildhall Museum, Newport
8   Roman Villa, Newport
9   Carisbrooke Castle
10 Isle of Wight Museum, Carisbrooke
11 Calbourne Water Mill
12 Needles Pleasure Park
13 Needles Old Battery & Viewpoint

North to South
14 Royal Yacht Squadron
15 Cowes Maritime Museum
16 Model Railway, Cowes
17 Sir Max Aitken Museum
18 Classic Boat Museum
19 Quay Arts, Newport
20 St. Catherine`s Lighthouse

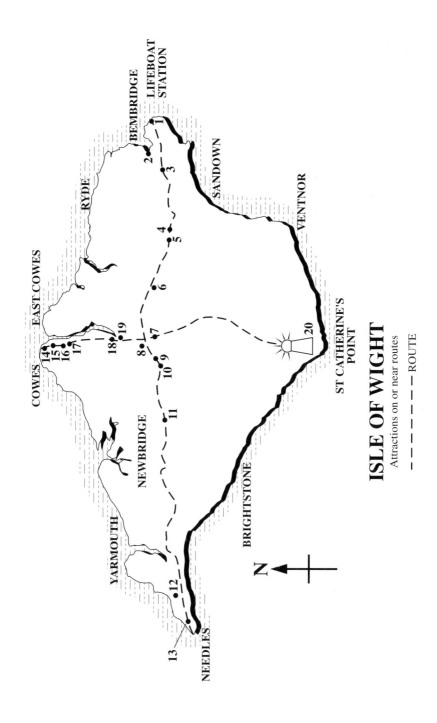

ISLE OF WIGHT

Attractions on or near routes

‐ ‐ ‐ ‐ ‐ ROUTE

Mileage between Prominent Landmarks

North to South	Miles	Km
Cowes (start) to Newport Centre	4.7	7.5
Newport Centre to Shide	0.9	1.5
Shide to Blackwater	1.2	2.0
Blackwater to St Catherine's Hill	6.2	10.0
St Catherine's Hill to Niton	2.2	3.6
Niton to St Catherine's Lighthouse	2.5	4.0
	17.7	**28.6**

East to West	Miles	Km
Bembridge L/B Station to Windmill	1.2	2.0
Windmill to Brading Church	2.6	4.1
Brading Church to Craft Village	5.7	9.2
Craft Village to Shide	3.0	4.8
Shide to Carisbrooke	1.5	2.4
Carisbrooke to Calbourne	4.6	7.4
Calbourne to Easton	6.4	10.3
Easton to The Needles	2.7	4.3
	27.7	**44.5**

Grid References

This section has been included to assist walkers, particularly those who have a G.P.S. to locate precise positions on route. You may also find it helpful generally to use in conjunction with the recommended O.S. map of the area.

North to South	G.R.
Cowes (start)	494966
Newport centre	498892
Barley Mow Pub, Shide	503881
Blackwater	506862
Little Birchmore	516853
A3020 Near Pagham	516837
Elliot's Hill	510834
East Appleford Farm	511827
Upper Appleford Farm	495801
St Catherine's Hill	495786
Turn off to Niton	500775
St Catherine's Point	499753

East to West	
Bembridge L/B Station	656881
Wall Lane Brading	614873
Lower Knighton Farm Ent.	570865
Approaching Craft Village	542864
Barley Mow Pub, Shide	503881
Car Park Carisbrooke Castle	485877
Frogland Copse	471861
Brighstone Forest (corner)	448855
Newbarn Farm	430870
Calbourne Mill	415868
Churchills Farm	397867
Near East Afton Fm Copse	366867
Tennyson Down	340858

Campsites on Route

1   Totland – Stoats Farm,Weston Lane,
    Tel: 01983 755258

2   East Cowes – Waverley Park Holiday Centre
    Tel: 01983 293452

3   Whitecliff Bay – Holiday Park, Bembridge
    Tel: 01983 872671

4   Newbridge – Orchards Holiday Camping & Caravan Park
    Tel: 01983 531331

5. St. Helens – Carpenters Farm
    Tel: 01983 872450

Star rating

1. **
2. **
3. ****
4. *****
5. **
6. ****

Additional campsite on public transport route.

6. Wootton Bridge – Kite Hill Farm
    Tel: 01983 882543

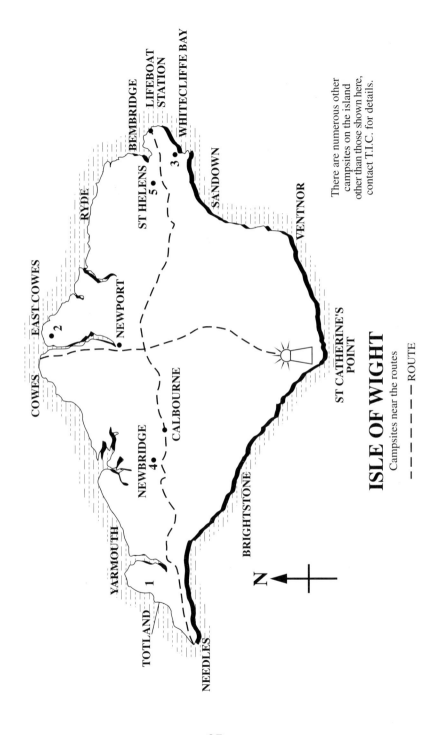

ISLE OF WIGHT

Campsites near the routes

– – – – – ROUTE

There are numerous other campsites on the island other than those shown here, contact T.I.C. for details.

Walking Times between Prominent Landmarks

North to South

Cowes to Newport	2hr	30min.
Newport to Shide		30min
Shide to Blackwater		35min
Blackwater to Kennerley Heath	1hr	15min
Ken. Hth. to Upp. Appleford Fm	2hrs	
Upper Appleford Farm to Niton	1hr	
Niton to St Catherine's Lighthouse		45min
	8hrs	**35min**

East to West

Bembridge L/B Station to Windmill		30min
Windmill to Brading Church		55min
Church to Craft Village	2hrs	
Craft Village to Shide	1hr	
Shide to Carisbrooke Castle		45min
Carisbrooke Castle to Calbourne	2hrs	
Calbourne to Easton	2hrs	30min
Easton to The Needles	1hr	20min
	11hrs	**0min**

A Selection of B&Bs on Route

North to South

Cowes area: -	Halcyone Villa	01983 291334
	Hillbrow Hotel	01983 297240
Newport: -	Magnolia Guesthouse	01983 529489
	Alvington Manor Farm	01983 523463
	(Carisbrooke)	
Niton: -	Pine Ridge Country House	01983 730802
	Lisle Combe	01983 852582

East to West

Bembridge: -	Xoron Floatel	01983 874596
	Harbour Farmhouse	01983 872610
Freshwater: -	The Wight Haven	01983 753184
	Field House	01983 754190

Should you require a greater selection of B&Bs
then contact the accommodation hotline 01983 813813

Tourist Information Centres

Ryde   -   Western Esplanade   01983 562905
Sandown -   8 High Street   01983 403886
Shanklin -   67 High Street   01983 862942
Ventnor -   34 High Street   01983 853625
Yarmouth -   The Quay   01983 760015
Cowes -   Fountain Quay   01983 291914
Newport -   High Street   01983 823366
Island Bus Information   01983 532373
Tourist Information Website www.islandbreaks.co.uk

The map required for both the routes described is: -
Ordnance Survey - Outdoor Leisure No.29
Isle of Wight   1:25000 scale

Public Houses on Route

The public houses mentioned below offer bar meals etc and/or have tables outside for patrons.

In Cowes, Newport, Bembridge, Freshwater and Niton there are numerous pubs so they are not mentioned individually. Those below are ones you pass directly on route.

North to South

Painters Arms   –   Cowes
Anchor Inn   -   Cowes
Harbour Lights   –   Cowes
The Duke of York   –   Cowes
Chequers Inn   –   Elliot's Hill
Buddle Inn   –   near St Catherine's Point
The Octopus Garden in Cowes (theme café)

East to West

The Bugle Inn   -   Brading
The White Lion   –   Craft Village
The Barley Mow   –   Shide
The Sun Inn   –   Calbourne

Post Walk

Have you enjoyed these walks? Have you found them a challenge? If so then consider walking The Isle of Wight Complete Coastal Footpath. This walk has fabulous views and dramatic scenery from start to finish.

The author has produced a number of other guides covering walks and challenges throughout Great Britain. These are shown at the front of this book or you can visit Challenge Publications website.

All books are available from most bookshops by quoting the ISBN No. if not in stock. Alternatively they are available direct from: -

Challenge Publications
7 Earlsmere Drive
Barnsley
S71 5HH

Visit our website and view each title: -
www.chall-pub.fsnet.co.uk

Will you accept the Challenge?